9/12

9/12: New York After

Eliot Weinberger

PRICKLY PARADIGM PRESS
CHICAGO

Prickly Paradigm Press, LLC
5629 South University Avenue
Chicago, Il 60637

www.prickly-paradigm.com

ISBN: 0-9717575-9-3
LCCN: 2002115990

Printed in the United States of America on acid-free
paper.

These essays were written for publication abroad. They appeared in *Lettre International* in Germany, *El Malpensante* in Colombia, *Tianya* in China, *D'Autres Espaces* on the web in France, *Magyar Lettre International* in Hungary, *Gazeta* in Poland, *Peterburg na Nevskom* and *Krasny* in Russia, *Lettera Internazionale* in Italy, *Yang* in (Flemish) Belgium, *Letras Libres* in Mexico and Spain, *Dialogos & Debates de Escola Paulista de Magistratura* in Brazil, *Letra Internacional* and *Lateral* in Spain, and *Tien Phong* and *Van Nghe Tre* in Vietnam. I am grateful to the many translators and editors involved.

In English, they circulated via e-mail among individuals, also turning up on websites and listservs. This is their first print publication in English.

I am a literary writer, and not a political analyst, an expert, an insider. The six essays should be taken as snapshots of what one person who reads the newspapers was thinking on six given days in recent history. Some of what I wrote has been overtaken by events or new information; in some cases, time has shifted emphases. I have, however, resisted the temptation to change or delete any statements in the original articles, other than a few stylistic alterations and the elimination of the inevitable repetitions that occur when independent articles are gathered together.

CONTENTS

PRELUDE: UN COUP D'ETAT TOUJOURS ABOLIRA LE HASARD

January 27, 2001: A novelist writes me: "Have you noticed that everyone is saying 'Happy New Year' sarcastically?" In the classified advertisements of the *New York Review of Books*, an academic couple, "in the wake of the national election," seeks employment in any other country. A Washington bank executive, whom I barely know, calls to ask what brand of cigarettes I smoke; she's decided to take up the habit again. Friends I meet on the street are less angry than dazed: marooned on the island of CNN for months, they now realize that no rescue ship is coming. The United States has suffered the first coup d'etat in its history.

Although no tanks circled the White House and no blood was shed, the word "coup" is only slightly hyperbolic. An illegality declared legal, a corrupt usurpation of power did indeed take place in the nation that imagines itself the world's beacon of freedom. Let me briefly review the story:

Al Gore received some 540,000 more votes than George W. Bush. Presidential elections, however, are determined by the archaic system of an Electoral College, to which each state sends representatives who vote according to the will of that state's voters, nearly always on a winner-takes-all basis. An eighteenth-century invention, the College was a last-minute political concession to Southern slave owners when the Constitution was written. Representatives were apportioned according to population; slaves, of course, could not vote, but they were considered to be three-fifths of a human in the calculations, thus increasing the populations of the slave states and the number of their representatives. It was also believed at the time, though this has been forgotten, that an elite of respectable electors would prevent the possibility of an inappropriate candidate being chosen by an unpredictable populace. The Founding Fathers had a limited enthusiasm for democracy.

Last November, as everyone now knows too well, the race was so close that the contest for the Electoral College depended on the votes in the state of Florida. The state is governed by George Bush's brother; its legislature is overwhelmingly Republican; and its Secretary of State, in charge of overseeing the election, was the co-chair of Florida's Bush for President campaign.

The state has long been notorious for payoffs under the palms, for a Southern provinciality without Southern hospitality, and a political demagoguery unsweetened by rhetorical flourishes. Predictably, the state's technicalities of voting varied widely. Wealthy white communities, more likely to vote for Bush, had modern voting machines. Black communities—and Bush nationally received even less black votes than Reagan—had antiquated machines which failed to count tens of thousands of votes. In a bizarre incident, thousands of elderly retired Jews, some of them Holocaust survivors, discovered that, because of a poorly designed ballot, they had mistakenly voted for Pat Buchanan, a minority party candidate who had expressed admiration for Hitler.

When the ballots were counted by the machines, Bush had won by 547 votes out of six million cast. In most American elections, such a small percentage automatically leads to a recount. Because the older machines are so inaccurate—even their inventor stated they fail to count 3-5% of the ballots—these recounts are usually done by hand.

The Republican Secretary of State refused to allow a recount and the Republican Florida legislature declared the election over. After weeks of maneuvers and reversals, the Gore campaign finally reached the Florida Supreme Court, which ordered a recount to begin. Republicans, in the hysterical surrealism of 24-hour news channels, relentlessly charged that the Democrats were trying to "steal" the election, and that humans could not count votes as "objectively" as machines—though hand counts are the practice in most states, including Bush's own Texas. More sinister, in the style of the Indian Congress Party and the Mexican PRI in the days when they ruled, the Republicans brought in paid demonstrators to disrupt the recount. These were housed at the Hilton Hotel, and the reigning Prince of Las Vegas, Wayne Newton, was flown in to serenade them at a special Thanksgiving dinner. Their demonstrations were so violent that the major potential source of Gore votes, the Miami-Dade County election office, was forced to shut down.

It was apparent to all that Gore would win the recount—according to the *Miami Herald*, a conservative newspaper, by at least 20,000 votes. So the Republicans went to the US Supreme Court. The deadline, under Florida law, for selecting the representatives to the Electoral College was December 12. On December 9—when, after endless legal battles, a system was finally in place to accurately count the votes—the Supreme Court stopped everything while it considered the case, on the bewildering grounds that a recount would cause "irreparable harm" to Bush by casting doubt on his victory. (The irreparable harm to Gore was not a consideration.) The vote was 5 to 4.

Supreme Court justices are appointed for life; seven of the nine had been appointed by Republican presidents. Among them, Sandra Day O'Connor had publicly stated that she was eager to retire, but would not do so if a Democrat were elected President. The wife of Clarence Thomas was already working on the Bush transition team, interviewing prospective employees for the new administration. The son of Antonin Scalia was a partner in the law firm representing Bush before the Court. Furthermore, Gore—never imagining they would decide the election—had promised in the campaign that he would appoint no Justices like the rigidly right-wing Thomas and Scalia; Bush had said they were exactly the kind of Justices he wanted. After all, his Dad had picked them.

At 10 p.m. on December 12, the Court, in another 5-4 decision, ruled against a recount for three reasons: there were only two hours left until the deadline—thanks to them!—therefore it was too late; the Florida Supreme Court had no jurisdiction over an election in Florida; and the recount was unconstitutional on the grounds that the various kinds of ballots and ways to count them violated the 14th Amendment of the Constitution, which guarantees "equal protection" for all citizens. Although the political bias and mendacity of these grounds were blatant, Bush was now legally and irrevocably the President.

The decision presented a practical dilemma. Every community in the US votes in a different way, with different ballots and different machines. Claiming that this difference was unconstitutional would clearly open the way to challenges to every future local and national election in the country. So the Court, even more astonishingly, also ruled that this constitutional violation only applied to this one election this one time in Florida.

The heart of the matter was articulated by Justice John Paul Stevens, in his dissenting opinion: "Although we may never know with complete certainty the identity of the winner in this year's presidential election, the identity of the loser is perfectly clear. It is the nation's confidence in this Court as an impartial guardian of the law." Americans, until December 12, had a blind faith in the Supreme Court: that no matter how corrupt or misguided the Executive or Legislative branches, somehow the lofty disinterest of Justice would prevail. This flagrant politicization of the Court is the greatest shock to the system since Watergate and Nixon's resignation. Its repercussions remain to be seen.

There are coups led by powerful individuals to install themselves, and coups where powerful forces install a figurehead. This American version is clearly the latter. In terms of previous government service, George W. Bush is the least qualified person ever to become President. For most of his life, he has been a type familiar to most of us from late adolescence: the bad-boy rich kid, the one who always has a new idea for a party or a prank. Grandson of a well-known Senator and Ambassador; son of a Congressman, Ambassador, CIA chief, Vice President, and President; his family connections got him into Yale and Harvard, where he spent his time on things like personally branding the initiates of his fraternity with a hot iron. Having graduated with the old Ivy League "Gentleman's C," the family secured him loans of millions of dollars from wealthy friends to start a series of businesses that all failed.

Success came when his father was elected President. A group of Texas millionaires decided to buy a mediocre baseball team, and they shrewdly installed the President's son as general manager. His mission was to persuade Texas to build a stadium for the team, entirely at taxpayers' expense. He succeeded, and a luxurious stadium was built, drawing the crowds. There was no doubt that Bush Jr. was a friendly and persuasive guy and, now that he had renounced his life-long excesses with alcohol and drugs and, as they say, let Jesus Christ into his heart, it was apparent on the golf courses where these decisions are made that Jr. would make a fine governor. A few months after his election, the baseball team was sold for a fortune, and the partners decided to give him many millions more—out of their own pockets—than his proper share. This was, of course, to reward his fine work, and not because he was the Governor with billions of dollars of contracts to award.

Bush may not be as stupid as he is tirelessly portrayed by cartoonists and television comedians—the most popular website of the moment is bushorchimp.com, comparative photographs of Bush and chimpanzees—but he may be the least curious person on earth. What is known about him is what he does not do. He does not read books, go to the movies, watch television, or listen to music of any kind. Despite his wealth, his only travels outside of the US have been a single beach vacation in Mexico, a short business trip to Saudi Arabia, and a summer vacation in China when his father was Ambassador, where he spent his time, reportedly, trying to "date Chinese women." During the five weeks when the election results were being contested, Bush remained secluded at his ranch, where he does not have a television. In other words, he was the one person in America not transfixed by the intricacies of the continuing story. Like a Chinese Emperor, his only source of information was what his ministers told him.

He is in bed by ten and takes long naps during the day; he always carries his beloved pillow with him. He likes to play Solitaire on a computer and something called Video Golf; his favorite food is a peanut butter sandwich. As Governor, he never read reports, but depended on summaries from assistants; details bore him. His difficulties with the English language are legendary, and there is a website, updated daily, of his mangled sentences. One journalist has speculated that he has a serious reading disability. Bush responded—and this is neither a joke nor apocryphal—"That woman who said I have dyslexia, I never even inter-viewed her!"

Yet, almost half of the voters (that is, 24% of the eligible voters, since only 50% actually voted) voted for him, thanks less to Bush's abilities than to Gore's inept-ness. Gore, in a neurotic insistence on disassociating himself from Clinton as a person—even though no one imagined he'd be having Monicas under his desk—refused to run on the eight Clinton-Gore years of economic prosperity. Nor did he ever bother to link Bush to the more unpopular aspects of the Republican Party, including their continual investigations of Clinton and the impeachment hearings—a six-year, slow-motion coup attempt that ultimately failed. The election, in the end, came down to who was perceived as a nicer guy. Gore had the mannerisms of a very nervous kindergarten teacher trying to be patient, while Bush was simply the guy who brings the beer to the party.

***

The last friendly dodo to be President, Ronald Reagan, was extreme in his servitude to what Eisenhower famously called the "military-industrial complex." Taxes on corporations and the rich were cut to almost nothing, defense spending escalated astronomically, the country went from a surplus to a trillion-dollar deficit, the middle class became poor and the poor were devastated. Bush, however, belongs to a new power structure, one that may well prove even more frightening: the military-industrial-Christian fundamentalist complex.

It is clear to everyone, left and right, that the least important man in the new administration is George W. Bush. His ignorance of all aspects of government and the world is so complete that he will be depending entirely on the advice of those in the senior positions. Many of them come from the Pentagon. His Vice President, Dick Cheney—universally seen as potentially the most powerful Vice President ever—was Bush Sr.'s Secretary of Defense during the Persian Gulf War. The Secretary of State, General Colin Powell, is a charismatic man with a moving personal story of rising from poverty, but it should not be forgotten that he helped cover up the My Lai massacre during the Vietnam War, oversaw the contras in Nicaragua, and led both the invasion of Panama and the Gulf War. (His appointment is also a violation of the unwritten rule that the State Department and the Pentagon, the diplomats and the generals, should remain separate to keep each other in check.) The Secretary of Defense, Donald Rumsfeld, is an old Cold Warrior who served in the same position under Gerald Ford in the 1970s and presumably has been defrosted from a cryogenic tank. He is well known for his opposition to all forms of arms control and enthusiasm for warfare conducted in outer space.

Their principal concerns will be to resurrect Reagan's science-fiction Star Wars defense system (against whom is unclear) and, equally terrifying, a return to Iraq. In their circles, the Gulf War is seen as a failure because it did not end with the assassination of Saddam Hussein. Bush must vindicate his father, and Cheney and Powell must vindicate themselves. On Day One of the Bush presidency, the front pages of the newspapers were already carrying stories about the buildup of "weapons of mass destruction" in Iraq. The only spontaneous news, of course, is earthquakes and plane crashes; the rest is always created by someone. If the economy sinks, as it probably will, a return to Iraq will certainly be the most expedient distraction.

Clinton's corporate friends tended to be from Wall Street or Hollywood; his last act as President was to pardon a long list of white-collar swindlers and thieves. But at least his corporate allies were environmentally benign. Bush's capitalist universe is the Texan world of oil, energy, mining and logging corporations.

Clinton had put a freeze on the economic exploitation of federal lands and declared millions of acres as protected wilderness areas. Bush has already announced his intention to open up those lands, most notably in Alaska, for mining and oil drilling. (Even his loyal brother is fighting him over plans to set up oil derricks off the Florida beaches.) While Bush was

Governor of Texas, Houston became the most polluted city in America because he instituted a policy of voluntary compliance with pollution regulations—and, needless to say, none of the heavy industries bothered to comply. His new Secretary of the Interior, Gayle Norton, refused to prosecute polluters when she was Attorney General of Colorado, enthusiastically supports mining and drilling in the national parks and voluntary compliance with environmental laws, does not believe that global warming is caused by humans and, most bizarrely, opposes regulations to prohibit lead in paint. The new head of the Environmental Protection Agency was the Governor of New Jersey, the second most polluted state (after Texas), where she also promoted voluntary compliance. The new Secretary of Labor is anti-union, and opposed to minimum wage laws and workplace safety regulations. The new Secretary of Energy is a former Senator who unsuccessfully introduced a bill to abolish the Department of Energy.

This is bad enough, but reminiscent of the Reagan-Bush era when, to take one of many examples, the person in charge of the protection of endangered species was a big-game hunter whose office was decorated with the heads of the exotic animals he'd shot. What will be new in the Bush Era is the power of the Christian Right.

During the election, Bush campaigned under the slogan "Compassionate Conservatism." This was generally understood to mean that he was a fiscal conservative with a social heart. Not once did the major media ever examine the meaning of the phrase. It was coined by a certain Marvin Olasky, a former Jewish Communist turned born-again Christian, editor of a fundamentalist weekly magazine, and the author of *Compassionate Conservatism*, and *The Tragedy of American Compassion*, as well as such tomes as *Prodigal Press: The Anti-Christian Bias of the Media* and *Telling the Truth: How to Revitalize Christian Journalism*. He is Bush's favorite, shall we say, "thinker," and his vision of compassionate conservatism is a very specific program: Government funds intended to help the poor, the sick, the illiterate, or the drug-addicted should be turned over to private Christian charities. Moreover, not all Christian charities—including some of the best-known—qualify. The only charities to receive these government funds are those where church attendance and classes in Bible study are required for any individuals receiving aid.

Bush attempted such a program in Texas, but was ultimately stopped by the courts. In the first week of his presidency, he has already announced similar plans. As a man who has publicly stated that those who do not believe in Jesus will go to Hell, it is natural for him to ignore the separation of church and state that is one of the foundations of American government.

As a candidate, he tended to keep his fundamentalist connections in the background, and to speak of himself as "a uniter, not a divider." He did, however, happily give a speech at the evangelical college, Bob Jones University, where students are expelled for dating a person of another race, and whose founder called Catholicism "the religion of the Antichrist and a

Satanic system."

As soon as he became President, however, he quickly dropped the pretense. His inauguration ceremony was unique in its specific references to Jesus Christ, rather than an ecumenical "God." For Attorney General, the most important domestic position in the cabinet—the one who selects all federal judges and prosecutors, and is responsible for enforcing such things as civil rights, environmental, and antitrust laws—he selected a former Governor and Senator, John Ashcroft, who regularly talks in tongues (as does Justice Clarence Thomas, the only black member of an all-white Pentecostal church) and is a pillar of Bob Jones University. Upon his election as Senator six years ago, Ashcroft poured cooking oil on his head, to anoint himself in the manner of Biblical kings. Last November, however, he was humiliatingly defeated in his reelection bid by a dead man—his opponent had died in a plane crash some weeks before.

Known as the most right-wing member of the Senate—even to the right of the notorious Jesse Helms—Ashcroft has publicly opposed all forms of contraception, the racial desegregation of schools, government support for the arts, pollution regulations, nuclear test-ban treaties, legal protections for women or homosexuals, government assistance to minorities, and even drunk driving laws. It is said that he believes that the murder of a doctor who performs abortions is justifiable homicide.

Ashcroft is not only opposed to any form of gun control, which might be expected, but he is also connected to an organization called Gunowners of

America, which believes that teachers should carry guns as a way of dealing with unruly students. Such views are not extreme around the Bush team, in a country where the leading cause of death among children is gunshot wounds, most of them accidental. As a Congressman, Vice President Cheney voted against a bill that would ban plastic guns, which pass unnoticed through airport metal detectors—a bill that was even supported by the National Rifle Association. A few years ago, after the student massacre at Columbine High School in Colorado, Tom DeLay, a former Texas bug extermi-nator who is now the most powerful man in Congress, said: "What do you expect, when these kids go to school and are taught that they're descended from a bunch of monkeys?"

Perhaps most bizarre of all, both Ashcroft and Interior Secretary Norton, although born and raised in the North and the West respectively, are obsessed with avenging the defeat of the South in the American Civil War. Ashcroft is associated with a neo-Confederate magazine called *Southern Partisan* that believes that the races were more harmonious under slavery, and that, among many other things, "Negroes, Asians, Orientals, Hispanics, Latins, and Eastern Europeans have no temperament for democracy." The magazine manufac-tures a t-shirt with a picture of Abraham Lincoln and the words "Sic Semper Tyrannis," which is what John Wilkes Booth shouted when he shot Lincoln. It is the t-shirt Timothy McVeigh was wearing on the day he blew up the government building in Oklahoma City.

Ashcroft is the person who will be responsible for enforcing the laws in the United States. A Supreme

Court that has not been so blatantly political since the nineteenth century will be responsible for the ultimate interpretation of those laws. A smiling rag doll is the President, surrounded by experienced and intelligent military men, industrialists, and Christian fundamentalists who, with a Republican majority in the Congress and no courts to stop them, can essentially do whatever they like. The United States, alas, is not a landlocked nation in the Himalayas or the Andes. Tremors here shake the world.

NEW YORK: THE DAY AFTER

September 12, 2001: I write in the limbo between the action and the reaction, knowing that the reactions and revelations to come will have already turned these words into a clipping from an old newspaper at the moment they first see print. This, then, is merely the record of a day, some notes from a temporal and emotional limbo.

And it is written from a geographical limbo, for where I live in New York, a mile or so north of the World Trade Center, is not the ruined war zone that is appearing on television, but a kind of quarantine zone. South of Canal Street, the buildings have been evacuated, telephones and electricity are out, and the air is

thick with rancid smoke and dust. Between Canal and
14th Street, which includes my neighborhood of
Greenwich Village, only residents are allowed to
enter—passing through a kind of Checkpoint Charlie,
manned by National Guardsmen wearing camouflage
suits and carrying rifles, slowly scrutinizing identification cards. There are no cars, no mail, no newspapers;
stores are closed; the telephones work erratically. At
least the air is clear. The wind is blowing south—
everyone has remarked how yesterday and today were
among the most beautiful days of the year—while
friends downwind in Brooklyn describe their neighbor-
hoods as Pompeiis of ash.

It is, of course, impossible to know what the
effects of yesterday's horror will be; whether it will
permanently alter the national psyche (if there is one)
or merely recede as yet another bundle of images from
yet another media spectacle. This is clearly the first
event since the rise of the omnipotence of mass media
that is larger than the media, that the media cannot
easily absorb and tame. If the media do succeed,
national life, beyond the personal tragedies, will
continue in its semi-hallucinatory state of continual
manufactured imagery. If they fail, something profound
may indeed change.

This is the first act of mass violence of this
scale to occur in the United States since the Civil War
of the 1860s. (Pearl Harbor, to which this has been
frequently compared—hyperbolically in terms of
consequences, but not unjustly in terms of tragic
surprise—was an attack on a military base in an
American colony.) We are now experiencing what the

rest of the world has known too often. It is the first time Americans have been killed by a "foreign" force in their own country since the Mexican War of the 1840s. (And for Mexicans, of course, the war took place in Mexico.) And it is the first genuine national shock since 1968: the assassinations of Robert Kennedy and Martin Luther King, followed by the riots at the Democratic Convention in Chicago. Despite the incessant attempts of television to fabricate disasters, no one in this country under the age of forty has ever experienced any serious threat to the general complacency.

The personal ramifications are nearly limitless. 50,000 people from all levels of society work in the World Trade Center and 150,000 visit it daily. Tens of millions throughout the country and the world will personally know (or know someone who knows) someone who died or miraculously escaped, or they will have their own memories of standing on the Observation Deck, looking out on New York harbor and the Statue of Liberty.

In contrast, the second attack site, the Pentagon, is a forbidden zone, as remote as a government building in Oklahoma City. Had only the Pentagon been hit, there would have been days of hand-wringing over the "blow to our national honor," but it too, like Oklahoma City, would have faded into merely another televised image. The Trade Center, however, is very real to a huge number of people; no sudden crisis, perhaps since the stock market crash of 1929, has so directly affected so many people in this country.

This shock has been compounded by a kind of incredulous despair that, on a national level, there is no one to reassure the citizens and guide them into a future that has become increasingly uncertain. The election (more accurately, the selection) of George W. Bush gravely and perhaps ineradicably undermined confidence in what was the last sacrosanct branch of government, the Supreme Court. Bush's response to yesterday's attacks has now—and perhaps forever—destroyed the last bits of hope that the Presidency would somehow mature him or bring to light some heretofore hidden abilities.

At the news of the attack, he left Florida, where he was visiting an elementary school, flew to a military base in Louisiana, and from there took refuge in the legendary underground bunker of the Strategic Air Command in Nebraska. (A place I haven't heard about since my Cold War childhood: there, we used to be told, the president and government leaders would retreat to keep the Free World free when the atomic bombs fell.) After a day of prevarication, Bush finally showed up in Washington, where he read, quite badly, a five-minute prepared speech, answered no questions from the press, and otherwise had no comments. As always, his face had an expression of utter confusion.

Bush was later followed by the Secretary of Defense, Donald Rumsfeld, whose bizarre press conference, evoking the inevitable Dr. Strangelove, was entirely devoted to security leaks. In a moment of national anxiety, and with hundreds dead in his own department, Rumsfeld devoted his time to complaints that during the Clinton administration people had become lax with classified documents. He grimly warned that sharing classified documents with those who are not authorized to see them could harm the brave men and women of the American armed forces, threatened that anyone sharing classified documents would be prosecuted to the full extent of the law, and urged Pentagon workers to inform superiors if they were aware of anyone sharing classified documents. When asked if the sharing of classified documents had in any way aided the terrorists, Rumsfeld said no and walked away.

No one has yet explained what exactly was on Rumsfeld's mind, but the logic of George Bush's seeming cowardice has received some ingenious explication. Today, administration officials claimed that the terrorist attack was actually an assassination attempt, that the airplane that struck the Pentagon was intended for the White House (but hit the Pentagon by mistake) and that the plane that had crashed in Pennsylvania was somehow supposed to crash into the president's jet, Air Force One. I happened to watch these pronouncements on television with a group of 13-year-olds; they all burst into derisive laughter.

In the postwar period, there have been presidents who have been considered, by the right or the left, as the incarnations of evil (most notably, Nixon and Clinton), but they were seen as evil geniuses. Bush is the first who is universally recognized as a fool. (Even his supporters maintain he's just an okay guy, but surrounded with excellent people.) That in a time of national crisis—a moment when, amidst waning government powers everywhere, government actually matters—the country is being led by a man laughed at by children may create psychic wounds as severe as those caused by the attack itself. It is no wonder that the response deep in America, far from the actual events, has been individualistically survivalist: a huge increase in gun sales, supermarkets emptied of canned goods and bottled water, and long lines at the gas pumps. When there's no government, it's every man for himself.

The perception of Bush's ineptitude has been further heightened by the remarkable performance of New York's Mayor Rudolf Giuliani. I write this with reluctance and amazement, having loathed Giuliani every minute of his eight years as mayor. He has been an ethnically divisive dictator whose ideology is, in his own words:

> Freedom is authority... the willingness of every single human being to cede to lawful authority a great deal of discretion about what you do and how you do it.

In this crisis, however, he has become the Mussolini who makes the trains run on time. Unlike his previous self, he has been completely open with the press, with whom he has been meeting every few hours. Unlike every other politician who is filling up television time, he has avoided nationalistic bombast and has limited himself to carefully outlining what the problems are and what solutions he is undertaking. Unlike Bush, he takes all questions, knows most of the answers in detail or explains why he does not. Giuliani's expertise has always been crisis management. His problem as mayor was that he treated day-to-day government as a continual crisis to be dealt with by a kind of martial law. Now that a real crisis has occurred, he has risen to the task.

The ruling myth in New York City in times of disaster or emergency has always been: "We're all in this together." This is once again the case, which Giuliani has recognized and turned to a general advantage. Unlike the rest of America, New Yorkers have not assuaged their common grief with nationalism and warmongering. They are not buying guns. In the largest Jewish city in the world, they are not attacking the Arabs who run small grocery stores in nearly every neighborhood. (Imagine if this had occurred in Paris or London.) Instead, their response has been an emotional outpouring of support for the rescue workers, firemen, medical workers, construction men, and police. When a convoy of relief teams passes by, people on the sidewalks applaud. So much food has been donated to them that officials are now sending out appeals to stop giving.

New Yorkers—contrary to their image, but not so surprising to anyone who lives here—have responded with a kind of secular *agape*, most evident in the candlelight vigils and makeshift shrines of candles, flowers, and photographs of the missing that are suddenly all over the city. Everyone is out on the streets, subdued and silent in the shock and mourning, but unmistakably there in the need to be around other people. Several times today, friends and even slight acquaintances I have run into—people who know that I don't live dangerously close to the Trade Center and that it would be extremely unlikely that I would have been there—have hugged me and said, "I'm so glad you're alive." It is not a sentiment directed to me as an individual so much as to me as a familiar face, a recognizable part of the community of the living.

I fear that this communal love will not be repeated in America at large, where the prevailing mood is already revenge. (Someone sent me an editorial from a newspaper in South Carolina that warns: "When they hit us with Pearl Harbor, we hit them back with Hiroshima.") If Bush shows any leadership at all, it will be in the name of war. He is surrounded by unrepentant Cold Warriors who, in the days before yesterday, had withdrawn the US from peace treaties and the negotiations between North and South Korea, had encouraged the nuclear buildup of India and (incredibly) China, are obsessed with the comic book Star Wars defense system, and, perhaps worst of all, had abandoned the Clinton project of disarming the stockpiles of nuclear weapons that remain from the breakup of the Soviet Union. (It is only a miracle that one of those bombs was not on one of those planes yesterday.)

Furthermore, ever since Reagan invaded Grenada—the only "war" since World War II the US actually won—it has become almost predictable that, when the economic news is bad, the President will launch military strikes (Panama, Iraq, Libya) as a domestic diversion and as a way to reverse waning personal popularity. The Bush plan of cutting taxes for the rich, increasing military spending, and sending everyone a check for $300 has turned a huge government surplus which might have been spent on the disastrous American health and education systems into a deficit; the economy at large is a mess. This terrorist attack has occurred in the first recession since Bush Sr. was president, and it is one full of grim forecasts for the future. Bush Jr.'s chances for reelection—the primary motivating force in American politics—have become dim. He needs a war.

And then there is the Curse of the Bushes, which is cowardice. Bush Sr. bailed out of the fighter plane he was piloting in World War II and the others on board died. Whether or not he was justified, he has been haunted by the charge of cowardice his whole life, and the Gulf War was, in many ways, his attempt to compensate. Even there, in the milieu of macho militarism that he inhabits, he was considered a coward for not "finishing the job" by invading Baghdad and killing Saddam Hussein. Bush Jr., like all of the most militant in the government today, evaded the Vietnam War. He too will feel the need to prove himself a man, and vindicate his father and himself, especially after his initial escape to the SAC bunker.

Worse, Bush will be goaded on by the likes of Condoleezza Rice, one of the most powerful and frightening people in the Bush administration. She is an unlikely, almost unbelievable, incarnation of the Prussian warrior caste ethos as an African-American woman: a bodybuilder and physical fitness fanatic who keeps a mirror on her desk so she can watch herself speak, an opponent of all forms of gun control, and one who, commenting on relief efforts in Kosovo, said that

American Marines were trained to wage war, not deliver powdered milk. In the context of Rice, Rumsfeld, and Vice President Cheney, among so many others, it is terrifying that General Colin Powell of the Gulf War and the My Lai massacre has become the last hope as a voice of reason in this government. He may be the only one who knows that Afghanistan—our most likely initial target—has always been a graveyard for imperial powers, from Alexander the Great to the British to the Russians.

Whether or not yesterday's attack leads to some kind of ground war or politically safer air strikes, and whether or not they in turn lead to further terrorism here, something profound has indeed changed. It is not so much a loss of innocence or security, as a loss of unreality. Since the election of Reagan in 1980, many now refer to the US as the Republic of Entertainment. It's quite true: less than half of its citizens bother to vote, but nearly all will dutifully line up to buy tickets to whatever blockbuster film has been hysterically promoted. (Films—particularly those this past summer—that no one actually enjoys, with huge box office sales the first weekend and little the following week.) Reagan, as everyone knows, was the master of transforming Washington into Hollywood, with his photo opportunities and careful scripts. Bush has taken this one step further: Whereas Reagan's scenarios were advertisements meant to promote what he was doing, Bush's are often heartwarming television vignettes that are the opposite of his actual policies. Thus we have had Bush in the forest extolling the beauty of the national parks, while opening them up for logging and mining, Bush reading to schoolchildren (as he was yesterday) while cutting the budgets for libraries. Or, my favorite Bush moment: a speech he gave to something called the Boys and Girls Clubs of America, a community service group, calling them exemplary of what makes America strong and free. The next day, his administration completely eliminated their government funds.

For the last twenty years, Americans have been living in a constant assault of media images, with a continual escalation of sensationalism—much as the Romans had to pour fish emulsion on their food to bring some taste to palates deadened by the lead in their water pipes. Violence has become grotesque, comedies depend on increasingly scatological stupidities which are mistaken for transgressions, adventure films have abandoned narrative to become theme parks offering a special effects thrill a second, corporations manufacture revolutionary rappers or angry white-boy rock groups, television turns the death of vaguely remembered celebrities into national days of mourning and the forecast of routine storms into dire warnings of potential disaster, and produces an unrelenting stream of Wagnerian tragedies out of the misfortunes of ordinary "real" people.

Of the many indelible images of the Trade Center attack, the one that I think, or hope, will have a permanent effect is that of the plane crashing into the tower. It was immediately perceived by everyone—it couldn't help but be—as a scene from a movie, one that even, by the second day, became available in different camera angles. America, as it has often been said, has become the place where the unreality of the media is the reigning reality, where everyday life is the self-conscious, ironic parody of what is seen on the various screens. But what will it mean when the realization sinks in that this ultimate simulacrum, the greatest special effect ever, led to the very real death of people one knows and the destruction of a place where one once stood?

Perhaps yesterday's attack will sink into collective amnesia, and we will return to the disaster movies and the late-night television comedians who, not surprisingly, are a major source of news for most Americans. For the moment, it is difficult to imagine a return to media fantasy as the opiate of the people. It has been telling that the television news, so accustomed to hyperbole, hasn't a clue how to deal with this story. They have produced it as television: dramatically lit, extreme close-up interviews with the relatives of victims, MTV-style montages set to music, handheld cameras following police and firemen in the manner of "reality" police shows. But unlike everything else that has appeared on television in decades, this story has a personal meaning to millions of its viewers. Despite the best efforts of television itself, this is something that so far has resisted becoming just another television show. Humankind can only bear so much unreality.

Meanwhile, the stories filter in of people I know slightly or well. A man who died in the hijacked plane that crashed into the Pentagon. A man who had a meeting at the Trade Center, but arrived twenty minutes late. A woman who was working on the 82nd floor of Tower 2, saw the plane hit Tower 1, began running down the stairwell, was below the floor where the second plane hit, kept running all 82 flights of stairs, and emerged unharmed. A photojournalist who had covered the wars in the Balkans and the Middle East, who heard the news, rushed to the scene to take pictures, and vanished. A woman who had stayed home sick. The high school students, two sisters, who had changed trains in the subway station below, ten minutes before, and continued on.

This morning, CNN had a banner that read: "MANHATTAN VIRTUALLY DESERTED." My son looked at me and said, "Hey, we're still here!"

NEW YORK: THREE WEEKS AFTER

October 2, 2001: In the Vietnam War days, there was a kitsch poster, adorned with doves and flowers, that read: "Suppose they gave a war and no one came?" Today's version, less wishful and oddly realistic, might say: "Suppose they declared a war and there was no place to have it?"

America is at war. It has suffered its worst—practically only—domestic civilian casualties since General Sherman burned Atlanta in the Civil War. Most of the country and both political parties have united behind a president who speaks in the language of religious zealots ("crusade"), cowboys ("Wanted: Dead or Alive"), and hunters ("smoke 'em out") to issue non-negotiable demands to foreign governments and openly advocates the overthrow of one of them. Hundreds of ordinary citizens have been arrested on the basis of their names or their appearance, and law enforcement agencies, invoking an emergency, are demanding the repeal of laws that protect civil liberties. Security at all public gathering places has created lines that stretch into waits of hours. Manufacturers of American flags, gas masks, and anti-anthrax medicines cannot meet the demands. Journalists at smaller newspapers have been fired for writing columns that disparaged the president, and some mild criticism from a television comedian was met with a stern rebuke from the White House that, in times such as these, "you should watch what you say." Mosques have been burned; thousands of Arab university students have returned home; hooligans in Arizona murdered a Sikh, though he was neither Arab nor Muslim, for the crime of wearing a turban. And, in a grotesque incident, a car full of white men in Oklahoma shot an American Indian woman, screaming, "Why don't you go back to your own country?"

Here in New York, there has been no violence, and the rage for revenge has been overwhelmed by the mourning for the six thousand or more dead and an outpouring of love for the firemen and other rescue workers, living or dead. The prevailing mood is the listlessness of shell shock, now called post-traumatic stress disorder, compounded by a dread of the future. Chance meetings on the street have the warmth of human contact—we're alive in this together—but on the telephone, people sound abstracted and very far away.

The universal adulation for Mayor Rudolf Giuliani in the first days of the crisis, however, is eroding swiftly, as his original security measures mutate into a kind of martial law. Giuliani must retire on January 1, thanks to the term limit laws which were passed, with his support, in the 1990s. But, riding the wave of his sudden popularity and in the unshakeable belief in his own indispensability, he has insisted on either repealing the law so he can run again or, at the least, being given an extra three months as mayor—a violation of the electoral process that is unprecedented in American history. Meanwhile, many days after the initial threat, irrational checkpoints have sprouted up around the city: a potential suicide bomber cannot walk to Wall Street, for example, but he can easily take a subway there. I must show identification whenever I walk down my own street, simply because there is a police station on the next block. (The barricades are manned by suntanned policemen from Florida, who were flown in as auxiliary troops, and who, examining the documents of passersby, are exhibiting an investigative zeal they notoriously lacked when the hijackers were living in their own state.) Most bizarrely, just a few days ago, Giuliani announced that it was forbidden for anyone, other than accredited members of the news media, to take photographs of the Trade Center rubble or the rescue operations—nearly three weeks after tens of thousands had gone to personally witness the devastation and, not knowing what else to do at such a scene, had taken a snapshot.

America is at war. The climate is one of fear, grief, uncertainty, unity, patriotism, suspicion of neighbors, hatred of the enemy—the war seems to have transformed every particle of ordinary life. And yet there is something missing, and that is war itself.

In the first days following the disaster, certain factions in the Bush administration urged him to immediately bomb Afghanistan, Iraq, Syria, and perhaps Iran, as punishment for harboring or supporting terrorists. A columnist, popular among the Bush crowd, wrote: "We know who the homicidal maniacs are. They are the ones cheering and dancing right now. We should invade their countries, kill their leaders, and convert them to Christianity." Bush himself, who had seemed hesitant and lost in the first few days of the crisis, appeared before Congress a changed and uncharacteristically resolute man. According to the *New York Times*:

> One of the president's close acquaintances outside the White House said Mr. Bush clearly feels he has encountered his reason for being, a conviction informed and shaped by the president's own strain of Christianity. "I think, in his frame, this is what God has asked him to do," the acquaintance said. "It offers him enormous clarity."

There was fear—and there still is fear—that Bush had become the mirror of Osama bin Laden, driven by God to slaughter. It seemed no coincidence that Bush used the word "crusade" for what America was about to do, and that bin Laden's umbrella organization for various terrorist groups was called the

International Islamic Front Against Jews and Crusaders. It appeared that a holy war was imminent.

And yet, three weeks later, nothing has happened. No one knows why, but it is assumed that the notorious prudence of Colin Powell—until now, a forgotten man in the Bush cabinet—and possibly some fatherly advice from George Bush Sr. have miraculously prevailed in Bush Jr.'s miasma of inexperience and ignorance. The problem, of course, is that a War on Terrorism is only a metaphor for a war, like the War on Drugs. It is a war with no enemy army and no military targets. The only possible military action would itself be another form of terrorism: bombing civilians in the hope that physical and psychological damage would lead to internal political change. It would be a terrorism, strangely, more in the style of the Algerians or the Irish or the Israelis or the Palestinians in their wars of independence, than of bin Laden, whose theatrical acts of carnage cannot hope to change minds or governments in the West, but which greatly amplify his reputation among certain sectors in the Muslim world.

Bush was quite right, in his address to Congress, when he, in passing, compared terrorists to the Mafia. The US spent most of the twentieth century fighting the Mafia—without, happily, carpetbombing Sicily—and largely without success. (The Mafia dwindled when it started sending its sons to Harvard Business School to learn how to manage the money.) The War on Drugs, thirty years and billions of dollars later, has merely led to a greater proliferation of drugs. Terrorism is a criminal, and not a military, activity, and it is always a scenario of disaster when the military replaces the police.

It is also a mistake to think of Muslim terrorism in strictly political terms. Bin Laden has, of course, stated political goals—withdrawal of the US military from Saudi Arabia, an end to the bombing of Iraq and to US support of Israel—but these are merely ornaments on something much larger. The terrorists are the anti-hero heroes of Radical Islam, and Radical Islam is the Islamic world's form and expression of Youth Culture.

The population has exploded throughout the Muslim world in the last fifty years; in some countries as much as sevenfold. In nearly all Muslim countries, the median age is 18, and a third of the population is between the ages of 15 and 30. There are hundreds of millions of young people with little education, without jobs and without the hope of jobs, packed into expanding and crumbling cities, living in countries ruled by oligarchies, whether secular or religious, of an educated and wealthy elite whose style of life is almost entirely unattainable for the masses. Thanks to television, the young are besieged with images of another world: not only the beautiful movie stars, but the unimaginable luxuries in the living rooms and kitchens of the supposedly ordinary families in comedy shows. Unlike Asia, where there are models nearby of nations that have achieved some semblance of that middle class glamor, in the Arab world there is only Israel, whose economic success has coincided with the repression of its Muslim inhabitants.

Radical Islam is a classic youth rebellion: total rejection of the values of one's parents; contempt for the dominant culture (which is perceived in stereotypes or abstractions); the invention of an entirely self-contained "alternate lifestyle" with strictly prescribed codes of belief, morals, knowledge, and even dress. Youth movements are fascinated with random and exaggerated violence: the Futurists' demands to burn down the museums; André Breton's description of the true Surrealist as the man who goes out in the street with a pistol and starts shooting; the Yippies' clarion call to go home and kill your parents. These are jokes and not jokes, and they accompany an iconoclastic adulation for those who do indeed commit such violence: the protagonists in bizarre murder cases, or fringe groups of political extremists, like the Weather Underground, the Baader Meinhof gang, the Brigato Rosso. In this sense, for the youths of Radical Islam, 2001 is their 1968, and the Trade Center attack a thrilling piece of spectacular political theater far beyond the imaginations of the Situationists. In this sense, the War on Terrorism will only end when this generation becomes middle-aged.

Like all youth movements, it represents a change of consciousness whose concrete manifestations are social rather than political. The Taliban, for example—and the word itself means "student"—much like the youth of the Chinese Cultural Revolution, with their public executions and punishments, have been terrifyingly effective in enforcing mores and customs—the growing of beards, the subjugation of women, the banning of music, television, and all things Western—but they haven't a clue how to feed their own people or rebuild the nation after its decades of war.

The response to youth movements tends to be political or military, and nearly always fails except when there is absolute internal repression (as in Tiananmen Square). In this case, the US government, having created the Taliban monster in its laboratories during the Cold War, is now about to create another monster, the Northern Alliance—a Taliban under another name—as the "freedom fighters" who will liberate the land. It never seems to learn the lesson of what the CIA calls "blowback": the unfortunate consequences of their liberatory intentions. It is a mistake the US has made many times, and it is a mistake to believe that the over-throw of the Taliban will weaken, rather than strengthen, Radical Islam as an international movement.

Meanwhile, three weeks later, we are still marooned in the limbo between the shock of the action and the uncertainty of the reaction. It is the mirror opposite of our continual bombing and starvation of Iraq, where nothing has been said while murderous things have been done. Now everything is said—there is no end to the bombast and threats—but nothing has happened. Hundreds have been arrested, but not a single one has been found who had any conscious connection to the hijacking plot. There is a universal demand for the head of bin Laden, but no evidence has been produced that he was involved, except ideologi-cally. There is a general panic about biological and chemical weapons, but no proof that other terrorist groups either have them or would be able to use them. Troopships and warplanes have been sent to the Middle East and Central Asia, but they remain, as of today, still mercifully idle.

***

Meanwhile, three weeks later, what has been most moving about the crisis has been a sense of community, of a common humanity, united not only by grief and outrage and love, but by storytelling. New York is the World City. Half of its inhabitants were born in another country, and most of the rest are their children. (A fact apparently not taken into consideration by the hijackers or the intellectuals abroad who have been bizarrely celebrating the hijackers: this blow against the American Empire killed many hundreds who were not Americans, and the many thousands of the living who are now jobless without benefits are mainly from Third World countries.) Anything that happens anywhere in the world, from a natural disaster to a political campaign, has repercussions here. So naturally an event of this magnitude here has been felt everywhere.

A national shock, like the Kennedy assassination, essentially led to personal variations of a single story: where I was when I heard the news. But the Trade Center attack has had expanding and tangling ramifications throughout the world. For the last three weeks, I've been spending my days listening to stories, not all of them tragic, and quite unlike the tales of extraordinary self-sacrifice and heroism that fill the newspapers:

The Belgian who celebrated his birthday on September 11 by taking his girlfriend to the seaside. Strolling through the town, they passed an appliance store with a wall of televisions in the window, all showing the jet crashing into the Twin Towers.

Assuming it was some disaster movie, they walked on.

The woman whose husband worked on the 80th floor of one of the towers and whose son was on a United flight from Newark to San Francisco. For many hours she did not know if her son had been the unwitting agent of her husband's death, and even worse, her last conversation with her husband had been a bitter argument. But her son had taken the flight that left an hour earlier, and the argument had caused her husband to arrive late for work.

The Indian who reported the rage at Bombay airport, where security forces were confiscating the large and potentially bomb-concealing jars and tins of homemade pickles, a source of family pride that Indians always carry back to their homes abroad or when visiting relatives. The heaps of pickle containers had turned the airport into a warehouse, unusually pungent.

The woman from an internet chat group of knitters, who told of a member in Australia who wanted to do something, realized that knitting is what she does best, and decided to knit a blanket to send to New York. Sitting on a bus in Adelaide, the passenger in the next seat wondered what she was making, and when it was explained, asked if she also could knit a few rows. Then other passengers asked, and the yarn was passed around. Finally the driver stopped the bus so that he too could work a little on the blanket.

The woman who was on a plane from Chicago to Denver when the Trade Center was hit. She watched the stewardesses suddenly going into the cockpit to speak to the pilots. They emerged weeping, whispering among themselves, then regained their composure and smilingly pushed the beverage cart down the aisle, dispensing drinks, without a word of explanation.

The American who had recently moved to a small village in France, where he had been met with the silent indifference of villagers anywhere. But on the day following the attack, most of the village came by, bringing food and flowers.

And, while the e-mails are full of falsified versions of the inevitable Nostradamus, one friend, who had turned to Herman Melville for a momentary escape, found these eerie words in the first chapter of *Moby Dick*:

> And, doubtless, my going on this whaling voyage, formed part of the grand programme of Providence that was drawn up a long time ago. It came in as a sort of brief interlude and solo between more extensive performances. I take it that this part of the bill must have run something like this:
> 'GRAND CONTESTED ELECTION FOR THE PRESIDENCY OF THE UNITED STATES.
> 'Whaling voyage by one Ishmael.
> 'BLOODY BATTLE IN AFFGHANISTAN.'

And another friend, reading Simone de Beauvoir's American diaries, found this entry for January 26, 1947:

> The sun is so beautiful, the waters of the Hudson so green that I take the boat that brings Midwestern tourists to the Statue of Liberty. But I don't get out

at the little island that looks like a small fort. I just want to see a view of the Battery as I've often seen it in the movies. I do see it. In the distance, its towers seem fragile. They rest so precisely on their vertical lines that the slightest shudder would knock them down like a house of cards. When the boat draws closer, their foundations seem firmer, but the fall line remains indelibly traced. What a field day a bomber would have!

NEW YORK: FOUR WEEKS AFTER (SHRAPNEL)

October 9, 2001: After ordering the bombing of
Afghanistan on October 7, George Bush went out on
the lawn to play with his dog and practice his golf
swings. Since September 11, he has maintained his
normal schedule of working until 6 p.m., four days a
week, and leaving at noon on Fridays for long week-
ends at his ranch or the Camp David retreat. Never has
an American president in a crisis looked so rested.

Along with the Tomahawk cruise missiles and the
bombs falling from F-14s and F-16s, B-52s, B-1s and
B-2s, the US also dropped 37,500 "Humanitarian Daily

Ration" packets, a single meal—complete with "moist towlettes"—in a country where four million are starving. These packets contained peanut butter and jelly sandwiches. Peanut butter sandwiches are iconic in the Bush family. Bush Jr. has stated that it is his favorite food. Bush Sr., shortly after he was elected president, outlined his vision of the future in these terms: "We need to keep America what a child once called 'the nearest thing to heaven.' And lots of sunshine, places to swim, and peanut butter sandwiches."

The original name of the mission, "Infinite Justice" was changed when Muslim clerics complained that only Allah may dispense infinite justice. The new name, "Enduring Freedom," was meant to proclaim that American freedom endures, but it now means that the Afghans must endure American freedom.

We are bombing Afghanistan in reprisal because it is believed that the terrorists who attacked the Trade Center and the Pentagon were housed and trained for their mission in Afghanistan. There is, as yet, no evidence for this assertion. What has been proven, however, is that the terrorists were housed and trained for their mission in Florida.

We are bombing Afghanistan to overthrow the repressive Taliban regime, which was of little interest to the US government on September 10. To this end, we are supporting the "freedom fighters" of the Northern Alliance, whose rule, from 1992 to 1996, was marked by internecine warfare, shifting alliances, betrayals, and the deaths of tens of thousands of civilians. Or we are supporting—and it would be laughable if it weren't so sad—the restoration of the King of Afghanistan, now 86 years old and never known for any leadership abilities. The Taliban brought an immediate order, however monstrous, to the country: It held public executions for social crimes, but it did not slaughter the masses. In brief: The Taliban is bad and the alternatives are worse.

In order to justify a military buildup and intervention, we have had to turn a small group of criminal outlaws into a full-scale enemy. The actual affinities of the hijackers are unknown, but it may be assumed that they were at least ideologically sympathetic to Osama bin Laden, the leader of one of many terrorist groups. Bin Laden, undoubtedly to his delight, has now been turned into the mastermind of all terrorist groups, tightly connected and organized as the al Qaeda network, which in turn has been portrayed as part and parcel of a national government, the Taliban, which has, although few, traditional military targets. With the invention of an enemy, the military must naturally exaggerate the capabilities of that enemy, a scenario familiar from the Cold War. The military cannot understand that against our billions of dollars of high-tech weaponry, the "enemy" attacked, and won the battle, with a handful of boxcutters. Thus the continual scare stories of chemical and biological weapons, for which there is no evidence that any terrorists either have them or would be able to deploy them.

Military reprisals for terrorist attacks (Libya, 1986; the Sudan and Afghanistan, 1998) killed civilians, strengthened anti-American sentiments, evidently did nothing to stop terrorism, and probably added new sympathizers to their ranks. Terrorism is a criminal and not a military activity; it cannot be erased, but it can be lessened with preventive security measures and with more attentive investigation, including the sharing of information among nations. For example, the 1993 bombing of the Trade Center might have been prevented if the FBI had translated the boxes of letters, documents, and tapes of conversations they already had in their possession. But these were in a foreign language, and the G-men couldn't be bothered.

An end to terrorism also depends on an impossibility, best articulated in a Utopian message written on a banner held by Pakistani demonstrators a few weeks ago: "America: Think About Why the World Hates You."

Rather than the attempt to apprehend the responsible criminals for trial in the World Court, we are now faced with a possible cascade of dominoes:

In Pakistan, General Musharraf has traded his support of US military intervention for the lifting of sanctions and the prospect of millions in foreign and military aid. Yet many members of the Pakistani army are veterans of the Afghan-Russian war, or their disciples, and are sympathetic to bin Laden. To avoid a coup d'etat or its own civil war, Musharraf will have to unite the country against a common enemy, which could only be India, with the battleground, as it has been for years, Kashmir. For its part, India, ruled by Hindu fundamentalists, has openly expressed its desire to follow the American example and attack Kashmiri terrorist groups which are housed and trained in Pakistan. Both countries, of course, have atomic bombs. (During the presidential campaign last year, Bush, when asked, could not name the leaders of Pakistan and India. Now, presumably, he knows.)

In Uzbekistan, which is admitting American troops, the Islamic Movement guerrillas trying to overthrow the dictatorial Islam Karimov, will surely gain followers, which could provoke Russian intervention, leading to another Chechnya. The American attacks will also rally forces in the continuing Chechnya war, as well as among the Muslims leading a separatist movement in China's Xinjiang province.

Palestinian police yesterday killed Palestinian youths demonstrating in support of bin Laden. The crumbling of Arafat's authority, already in progress, will lead to the strengthening of militarist groups, which in turn will provoke further interventions by the terrifying Ariel Sharon, who has already charged the US with "appeasement" of the Arabs.

Throughout the Muslim world, the specter of American military might slaughtering helpless Afghan peasants will only fuel the rage of the youths of Radical Islam, threatening regimes from the autocratic Saudi Arabia, which bin Laden wants to overthrow for allowing the American military on sacred land, to Egypt and Turkey, which are already under threat from fundamentalist movements.

Meanwhile, the FBI, with their usual sensitivity to the public, has stated that there is now a "100% certainty" of terrorist reprisals in the US.

The War on Terrorism will be orchestrated by Vice President Cheney in the same manner in which he ran the Gulf War: in secrecy and with total control of the media. (At his press conference yesterday, Secretary of Defense Rumsfeld three times told reporters not to quote him, even though the press conference was being broadcast live on CNN.) American successes will be exaggerated—the Gulf War was reminiscent of Orwell's *1984* in its daily pronouncements of victorious triumph—but there is hope that the Western media, at least outside of the US, will not allow itself to be fooled again, and what has changed since the Gulf War is the rise of the internet as a source of instant oppositional information. It remains to be seen whether the Taliban has the media savvy to appeal to the world's sympathies by magnifying their own casualties, or whether they will stubbornly maintain the machismo of pretending that they have not been harmed at all.

Bin Laden, however, has unexpectedly turned out to be a media genius. He has managed to indeed "terrorize" the West, and greatly magnify the perception of his actual power—which, before now, was small—by planning (or capitalizing on) the transformation of a Hollywood disaster-movie image into an unbearable reality. On the other side, his release of a tape of himself two days ago, immediately following the initiation of the bombing, was a brilliant evocation of a revered figure in Muslim tradition: the wise and ascetic saint in his cave. His message, in image and word, had the directness of television advertising, and would be impossible to refute with an equal directness: We are simple men of the faith and they are the monsters who bombed Hiroshima and have killed a million children in Iraq and will kill us now in Afghanistan.

Bin Laden, in the tape, recalled the defeat of the Ottoman Empire. He was followed by his chief tactician, Ayman al Zawahiri of the Egyptian Islamic Jihad, who invoked the "tragedy of al Andalus," the expulsion of the Moors from Spain. One side believes this war began four weeks ago; the other that it is five hundred years old.

There is something more: I knew two people who died on September 11; many others were the friends of friends. Until now, they and the six thousand others were the innocent victims of an unimaginably enormous crime. But, as I watched the scenes of demonstrations around the world, I realized that they, in death, had been transformed into something else. Now they are war casualties, numbers in an increasing body count, as anonymous as the Afghans who will die from the American bombardment. No longer murder victims, they will now be portrayed, by both sides, as having died for a cause. By avenging their deaths with more deaths, Bush and Cheney and Rumsfeld and Rice and Powell are murdering the identities and, above all, the innocence of our own dead as they murder abroad.

NEW YORK: ONE YEAR AFTER

September 1, 2002: On the verge of the first anniversary, and a commemorative media frenzy that may send the country into diabetic shock, one can either retreat to the hills like a Chinese sage, or contemplate, for a moment, from near or far, Ground Zero.

There is nothing there. The rubble has been scraped clean, so that the area now truly resembles its eponym, the Ground Zero of a nuclear attack; the empty air once occupied by the towers is almost palpable. And yet the utter nothingness of the scene is calming: a refuge of silence, an anti-memorial that is the best possible memorial, a still center around which swirls a world and a year of continual and continually mutating madnesses.

Since Sept. 11, the American national obsession has been the delineation of how "we" are different. It seems that every magazine or newspaper article, regardless of subject—marital relations, video games, summer vacations, the new fiction—must now include at least one paragraph demonstrating how its subject, or the future of its subject, has been irrevocably transformed by that terrible day.

"We" has always been a useless generalization in a nation inhabited by a plurality of peoples who have almost nothing in common except for their taste in certain consumer goods and fast food—a taste now shared by hundreds of millions in other countries who are supposedly not "us." In fact, the word "American," when applied to anything other than the policies of the US government, is nearly always meaningless: there are too many exceptions to the rule.

Nevertheless, to indulge in this first person plural, it is difficult to see how the artifacts and attitudes of Americans have changed at all since Sept. 11. To take an obvious example: More people than ever went to the movies this summer to watch things getting blown up—even, in the case of *Spiderman*, blown up in New York—movies that, according to the commentators on Sept. 12, would never be made again, for reality had overtaken illusion. But somehow, despite disaster and expert readings of the zeitgeist, life and *Spiderman* have a way of going on.

And yet, something is indeed different. To put it simply, "we" are the same, but we are nervous wrecks. In the last year, Americans have become like the novitiates in cults, kept awake and in a state of constant distraction. Or, more precisely, like the captured spy in 1960s movies, whose form of torture is to be tied to a chair in a small room with blaring music and images flashing on the walls.

Two powerful forces have combined to drive Americans crazy. On one side, the White House Team. (In this case one cannot, as is usual, personify and refer to an administration by the name of its leader, for George W. Bush has exactly the same relationship to the policies of his government as Britney Spears does to the operations of the Pepsi corporation). Like all despotic governments—and I do not use the word lightly—they have recognized that the best way to solidify popular support is by exaggerating internal and external threats to the society. On the other side, there is the hyperbolic and hysterical 24-hour news media, continually in need of further sensationalism to keep their audience frozen before the television. Together, the two have created a kind of techno rave of the disturbing and the frightening, with each new artificial panic blending into the next and erasing the memory of the previous one.

We've been driven crazy because every two or three weeks for many months, the FBI or the bizarre Christian fundamentalist Attorney General, John Ashcroft, would announce that another terrorist attack was "imminent" and a "certainty" in the next few days, or this weekend, or next week. So that no American would feel complacent, the targets were spread around the country: the Golden Gate Bridge, the Sears Tower, the Lincoln Memorial, Disney World, the Liberty Bell, and even, god forbid, Universal Studios.

Ashcroft, having apparently watched *The Manchurian Candidate* too many times, periodically warned of "sleeper cells" of al Qaeda terrorists, living anonymously, maybe right next door, who could be awakened at any moment. Nearly every day, airports were evacuated, malls emptied, traffic stalled for hours crawling through checkpoints.

We've been driven crazy because, in the first weeks after Sept. 11, the media endlessly fixated on the possibilities and consequences of terrorist biological weapon attacks, and specifically on anthrax. Predictably, this led to some thrill-seeking loner—a stock character in America—sending anthrax spores through the mail, spreading fear among all those citizens not in immediate proximity to historical monuments and theme parks. Equally predictably, the White House Team and the subservient media pronounced this to be the work of Arab terrorists, although it was obvious from the first day that the poisoned letters were being sent by one of our own Timothy McVeigh or Unabomber types—an international terrorist might release anthrax spores in the Washington metro, but he wouldn't mail them to a celebrity gossip tabloid popular in the supermarkets of the American provinces. (And we now know that the White House Team was so obsessed with finding an Iraqi connection that it actually forbade the FBI—which is inept enough without outside help—from pursuing domestic leads.) It still takes months for a letter sent to any branch of the government to arrive, for all their mail, like an American dinner, must be cooked in a microwave.

We've been driven crazy because the secret arrest and deportation without trial of thousands of men (the exact number is unknown) for the crime of being Middle Eastern or dark skinned or speaking a foreign language in a public place—a group that included Israeli Jews and Indian Sikhs—was terrifying not only for Muslim Americans, but for millions of legal and illegal residents of non-European origin. Among the Latin Americans I talked with—poor people with a very hazy idea of Muslims, but an encyclopedic knowledge of immigration laws and practices—there was a general belief that it would be "first them, and then us."

We've been driven crazy because the secret arrests; the pronouncements by Ashcroft that any criticism of the government was an act of treason; the internet postings of lists of university professors who criticized the government; the Presidential proposal to create an army of millions of government informers, composed of postmen, gas and electric meter readers, pizza delivery men, and anybody else who rings the doorbell; and the warnings from that Grim Reaper, Secretary of Defense Donald Rumsfeld (whom Henry Kissinger, of all people, once called "the scariest person I've ever met") about traitors among us leaking classified information, combined to provoke fears of reprisal among those with opinions to express, whether publicly or privately. After all, the bedrock of American democracy is, in theory, freedom of speech. In practice, this has meant that anyone can say anything because no one is listening. Suddenly there was the possibility that people like Ashcroft were listening, and that critics would be turned into dissidents, facing tangible repercussions for their intangible ideas.

We've been driven crazy by the wars, actual and threatened. It has been forgotten that on Sept. 10, Bush was an extremely unpopular president. The economic boom of the Clinton years was crashing, and he was generally seen as a fool, the butt of nightly jokes by television comedians; an automaton controlled by his Dr. Mabuse/Dr. No/Dr. Evil vice president, Dick Cheney; a president who hadn't even been elected, but had taken office in a kind of judicial coup d'etat. The only hope for Bush was a war to rally the nation, as his father had done in his own economic crisis, and it is evident that, if Sept. 11 hadn't occurred, the US would have invaded Iraq late in the year. The Team began talking about it on the first day of the Bush presidency, but they needed to put the administration in place and wait for cooler weather in the desert.

Sept. 11 gave them an alternate opportunity. Instead of treating the attack—as was done in Europe—as a monstrous crime whose perpetrators were dead but whose accomplices needed to be apprehended, it was immediately categorized as an act of war, a new Pearl Harbor, which it clearly was not. (War, as has often been said, is politics or business by other means: the attempted coercion of the other side to accept one's policies or products or sovereignty. Al Qaeda, like all revolutionary youth movements, is more concerned with consciousness than political realities, and the Trade Center attack was a kind of grotesque advertisement for itself.) In the absence of a tangible enemy with whom to wage war, the Team quickly confused al Qaeda with the Taliban in the public mind, launched the War on Terrorism—turning a metaphor, or an advertising slogan, into a grotesque reality— proclaimed new and thrilling victories every day, and probably slaughtered many more innocent people than died on Sept. 11.

As for Osama bin Laden or any other important al Qaeda member, the War on Terrorism never did, in Bush's famous John Wayne words, "smoke 'em out and hunt 'em down." But no matter: The media were delighted with the capture of a pathetic California teenager, whom they quickly named "The Rat" as they clamored for his execution, until his family hired some expensive lawyers—the American Way of Justice—and saved his life. But no matter: Ashcroft soon interrupted television programs to announce via satellite from Moscow the sensational arrest of a sinister-looking man with an Arab name who was about to explode radioac- tive "dirty" bombs in unnamed American cities. This led to days of televised delirium about how easy it is to make such bombs and their potential death tolls and how we can or cannot protect ourselves, until it was revealed that the nefarious dirty bomber was a Puerto Rican street gang member from Chicago who had converted to Islam in prison, and whose sinister plot had consisted entirely of looking up "radioactive bomb" on an internet search engine.

But no matter: With nothing panic-inducing coming from Afghanistan, the White House Team scanned the horizon for other places to imagine waging war. Indonesia? The Philippines? Syria? Plans were proposed, gloated over, and forgotten. Then, having already refused to support the negotiations, initiated by Clinton, between North and South Korea, the Team suddenly, out of nowhere and on the basis of nothing, began threatening to drop the Big One on North Korea—the first time the US government has ever spoken of a "preemptive first strike" with a nuclear weapon. This was followed by Bush's famous "Axis of Evil" speech—the Axis, as you may have forgotten, consisted of the closely allied nations of Iran, Iraq, and North Korea, but somehow omitted the Vandals, the Huns, and the Visigoths—which was so scary that my children seriously asked whether it wasn't a good idea to move to Costa Rica. And now of course the Team is waging a weird simulacrum of war in Iraq, in the manner of the tactical board games that geeks used to play before the Age of Nintendo: Every day they announce different battle strategies, complete with maps, which are followed by explanations—apparently based on telepathy—of what Saddam's defensive strategies will be.

But most of all, more than the nightmares of sleepwalking terrorists, secret police, nuclear strikes, and the junk mail of doom, in the last year we've been driven crazy by money. During the Clinton years, for the first time, the middle class put most of their savings—particularly their retirement pension savings—in the stock market. Now they have lost half of it—and in many cases much more than half. And the collapse of the stock market has meant that many millions have either lost their jobs or must work at severely reduced wages. This, more than anything, has been devastating in a country founded on the "pursuit of happiness" and the dream of the bright future. Typically, the White House Team's solution to this crisis is to cut the taxes of those who earn more than $2 million a year. And they not only want to cut corporate taxes, but also make the cuts retroactive so that the corporations would get back the money they'd paid over the last twelve years. (As there is still supposedly an opposition party called the Democrats, they prudently chose a dozen, and not fifty or a hundred years.)

Is it possible to understand the United States? Europeans tend to think of it merely as a richer, more vulgar, and more violent version of Europe. But the two have little in common, other than large numbers of white people. The United States is a Banana Republic with a lot of money. It is perhaps the most perfect form of Banana Republic. Its generals do not have to seize power, or even concern themselves with those tedious, domestic, non-military matters for, regardless of who the ostensible leader of the government is, the generals always get what they want: lots and lots of toys to play with. (Often the Congress even gives them toys they don't want.) Moreover, like the generals of a Banana Republic, they have no great desire—since the Vietnam War—to kill people with those toys, as that might mean that some of their own boys would be killed. They're equipment fetishists, and all they want is the latest hardware and elaborate maneuvers in which to try it out. Their kind of war is Grenada, and their reluctance to go to war continues to be the greatest force for peace in the nation.

If one considers so-called "intelligence" as part of defense, approximately two-thirds of the American tax dollar goes to the generals. That naturally leaves very little for anything else, which is why the US, in terms of infrastructure and general well-being, is the Banana Republic of the industrialized nations, with 25% of its children living in poverty, the worst education system, the worst mass transit, no socialized medicine, the highest rates of illiteracy and infant mortality and teenage pregnancy, homeless millions, and small cities that look as though they've just been through the plague.

Like that of any Banana Republic, the government is largely controlled by the rich. This has become even more exaggerated since the rise of the dominance of television in American politics. One now needs vast amounts of money to buy television advertisements in order to get elected—a minor position in local government costs a million dollars, the last presidential campaign cost a billion—and those who manage to get elected must then spend the majority of their time raising the money for their reelections. That money, needless to say, comes from the people or corporations who have it, and those people or corporations, needless to say, expect things in return. (American politics would be completely transformed overnight if television campaign advertisements were banned, as they are in most of the world, but that would entail the system voluntarily deciding to destroy itself.)

Nevertheless, before the Age of Bush, there was always the assumption that a few things had to be done for the good of the people who are actually casting the votes. This was partially because one needed those votes again, and partially because the non-elected government officials tended to come from the ranks of civil servants who, after all, had decided to dedicate their lives to serving the citizens. But Banana Republics are sometimes ripe and sometimes rotten, and this White House Team is something entirely new. Most of them, having worked for Bush Sr., spent the Clinton years in the executive offices of oil, energy, and pharmaceutical corporations. The Chief of Staff was the primary lobbyist in Washington for the auto industry against pollution controls, and Condoleezza Rice—the Team's own Xena the Warrior—even has an oil tanker named after her. In the year 2000 alone, the year before they joined Junior's Board of Directors, nearly every one of them—including Colin Powell—earned between $20 and $40 million. Most have a net worth of at least $100 million, and many have much more. Considering that Bush wasn't even elected, his Team represents a corporate hostile takeover of the US government.

Let us drill into the skull of George W. Bush. His ignorance of almost everything in the world borders on the pathological. It is nearly impossible to imagine a wealthy man from an old and distinguished New England family, educated at Andover, Yale, and Harvard, who not only never thought to visit Paris, but on his first trip there this year could declare: "Jacques [Chirac] tells me the food is fantastic here, and I'm going to find out." The person he resembles most is Osama bin Laden: both the formerly dissolute sons of rich families; both called by the One God (who seems to be contradicting Himself); both cut off from the world, one in a cave and one on a ranch in the middle of nowhere; one who reads no books and the other who presumably reads one book. Is it any wonder that their families are business partners and friends? [On Sept. 11, the only non-military plane allowed to fly was a chartered jet that left Logan Airport in Boston—the same as the hijackers—carrying eighty members of the bin Laden family back to Saudi Arabia. The conspiracy-minded may wonder how this was arranged so quickly, and before the identities, let alone the allegiances, of the hijackers were known. The link to Osama was only presumed in the following days, and only partially confirmed months later.] Bush has spent his entire life in a world as provincial as that of the House of Saud (and evidently one where France is never mentioned): a tiny circle of Texas oil and energy millionaires who repeatedly rescued him from his financial disasters because he was the President's son and a nice guy and one of them.

In the manner of patrician families, he believes, as his father did, that he and his Team know what's best for the country and the world, and they have no patience for tiresome other opinions. When they had to formulate an energy policy for the administration, they assembled a group of energy corporation executives, without bothering to include even a token environmentalist or consumer advocate or labor leader; and then they refused to release the proceedings. When they recently organized a conference to discuss the economic crisis, only large contributors to the Republican Party and small-town Republican businessmen were invited. The Team believes in Secret Government, which has been epitomized by the bizarre disappearances of Vice President Cheney-Mabuse—supposedly to protect him from terrorists, though the Team's spokesperson Bush makes frequent public appearances—which would always lead to speculation that he was dead, until he (or perhaps a double) miraculously turned up again on television. This is why they couldn't care less if the rest of the world—even their own generals—is opposed to an invasion of Iraq. They know that men must do what they have to do. On Rumsfeld's desk is a plaque with these words from that big game and small nation hunter, Theodore Roosevelt: "Aggressive fighting for the right is the noblest sport the world affords."

If you drill into Bush's skull, what you mainly find is a pool of oil. It's difficult to understand Bush—especially when he speaks—but it is somewhat easier if one realizes that he sees the whole world exclusively in terms of the production and consumption of oil. Long before Sept. 11 he was discussing the overthrow of the Taliban so that Unocal could build a pipeline through Afghanistan from Kazakhstan to Pakistan. [The current US Special Envoy to Afghanistan—the equivalent of ambassador—was Unocal's chief consultant on the project. The so-called President of Afghanistan, Hamid Karzai, is a former Unocal executive.] The only country in the Western Hemisphere that has attracted his attention is Venezuela, where he tried to overthrow Hugo Chavez, because that's where the oil is. He has no interest in Palestine and Israel, because they have no oil. Libya is notably not a member of the Axis of Evil, because Qaddafi has made arrangements with the oil companies. Europe is a petty annoyance that doesn't even have any oil; Russia has oil and Bush said that when he looked deep into Putin's eyes he knew he was a good man. The totalitarian terrorist-supporting nation of Saudi Arabia is our friend because the oil flows; the totalitarian terrorist-supporting nation of Iraq is our enemy because the oil isn't flowing as it should.

But if you drill to the core of George W. Bush's being, there is something else, something that seems so hyperbolic, that so smacks of the clichés of old Communist propaganda, that it is hardly believable. And yet the evidence of his term as the Governor of Texas, and the daily evidence of his presidency proves that it is true. Once one clears away the rhetoric that he is handed to read out loud, it is apparent that Bush believes that his role, his only role, as President of the United States is to help his closest friends.

When he was Governor, he took over countless public funds and operations, eliminated the public oversight committees, and simply handed the money or the work to his golf buddies; laws were changed strictly for their benefit. Now that he is President, his Team has completely restaffed the middle level of the bureau-cracy—the place where the day-to-day and tangible laws are effected—and they, in turn, have rewritten innumerable rules and regulations, not to help big business in general, as might be expected, but as specific gifts to the oil, energy, mining, logging, and pharma-ceutical corporations run by the Bush crowd. Every day, in the back pages of the newspaper, there is yet another story that strains credulity. I'll mention only two: No doubt at the urging of Rumsfeld, a former pharmaceutical CEO, the Team eliminated the law that required drug companies to perform separate tests on medicine that is prescribed for children—why should they spend the money? And, only a few days after it came out in the press that there were massive Enron-style accounting "irregularities" in the Halliburton Corporation when Cheney was its CEO—which he ran so badly that they paid him $45 million to leave—the White House announced that the five-year, $1.5 billion project to expand and maintain the prison at Guantanamo Bay (in expectation of more Afghan peasants to be held forever without trial) was awarded to a division of the Halliburton Corporation. One must go back to the nineteenth century to find this level of oblivious corruption in the White House.

After Sept. 11, many intellectuals abroad, and many others, privately or publicly, celebrated the attack—after some perfunctory handwringing about loss of life—as a humiliating blow against the American Empire, and a just reward for the decades of American hegemony and aggression. One year after, it is worth remembering the concrete facts of the consequences of that day:

Because the attack happened early in the morning, the nearly 3,000 people who died were generally of three types: first, poor people—most of them black, Hispanic, or recent immigrants—who worked as janitors, handymen, food deliverers, and so on, in the towers and the adjoining buildings; second, low-ranking white-collar workers: the secretaries and junior managers who had to be in the office before the bosses arrived; and third, firemen, policemen, and other rescue workers. Very few titans of capitalism or people in power died that day.

The devastation of the downtown business area and the subsequent collapse of the tourist industry caused at least 100,000 people, most of them poor, to lose their jobs.

The secret arrests and deportations ruined the lives of some thousands of Muslim men and their families—not a single one of whom was proven to have had any connection to the hijackings—and brought continuing fear to hundreds of thousands of others.

Immigration to the US has essentially ground to a halt, with the consequent hardships to countless divided families, and the millions in Third World countries who depend on the money earned by relatives in the US. Among many other specific cases, 100,000 Mexican and Canadian students who commuted to colleges and universities across the border can no longer attend classes; for the Mexicans especially, this education was their hope for decent employment.

Thousands of innocent people in Afghanistan are dead, and tens of thousands displaced. The potential deaths in Iraq or elsewhere remain to be seen.

George W. Bush, a fool on Sept. 10, became a powerful and popular leader. He and his Team are the most globally frightening White House in modern times—far more frightening than Nixon or Reagan—and they can now do anything they want. Hardly a blow against the Empire, the Trade Center attack created one of the most arrogant and aggressive administrations in American history, one that has already demonstrated its impatience with, or repugnance for, such foundations of American democracy as free speech, open elections at home and abroad, due process of law, and the separation of church and state. And their actions will have incalculable ramifications, large and small, throughout the world, from the acceleration of global warming to the end of birth control programs in Third World villages.

For the White House Team, the hijacked planes were a blessing from the sky.

A few days ago, a man listed as one of the Sept. 11 dead was discovered in a psychiatric hospital, a total amnesiac who has no idea what happened to him or what has happened since. On the same day, George W. Bush told an interviewer what the "saddest thing" has been about his presidency: He now only has time to jog three miles a day.

NEW YORK: SIXTEEN MONTHS AFTER

January 11, 2003: For years they'll be debating the future of the empty pit where the World Trade Center once stood, with fantastic or hideous proposals of gardens in the sky or indoor lakes or threatening tic-tac-toe-shaped fortresses. But at the moment, the only thing certain is the fate of the actual towers themselves. The scrap steel will be shipped from the Fresh Kills landfill in Staten Island to the Grumman shipyard in Trent Lott's fiefdom of Pascagoula, Mississippi. There, it will be melted down and turned into the "New York," an $800 million "state of the art" amphibious assault ship. In Bush America, every ploughshare must be beaten into a sword.

War and war and war. 150,000 troops are massed in the surrounds of Iraq, many of them reservists pulled from their normal lives, preparing for what the Pentagon is already declaring the "greatest precision-bombing aerial assault in history," to be followed by an invasion which the United Nations estimates will cause 500,000 casualties. There are troops or "advisers" in India, Pakistan, Uzbekistan, Kyrgyzstan, Georgia, the Philippines, Colombia... and speculation that Iraq is merely a stop on the road to Iran.

Military operations in Afghanistan are continuing at a cost of a billion dollars a month—compared to the $25 million a month the US is spending there on humanitarian aid, most of it paying for the offices and maintenance of the aid workers, or vanishing into the crevices of local corruption. Helmeted and armored Special Forces troops still move like Robocop through the villages, past the hundreds of thousands of displaced peasants trying to survive the winter.

This year, the Pentagon budget will increase by $38 billion to almost $400 billion. The increase alone is practically the entire budget of the second biggest military spender, China. Meanwhile, millions of Americans have lost their jobs or have had their salaries greatly reduced. There are schools around the country that will be closing a month early this year because of budget cuts, further evidence of the theory that Republicans never allot any money for education in order to keep the electorate stupid so that they'll vote for Republicans.

Everything is war and war, the talk of war, while the real, declared war—the War on Terrorism—is a complete failure. It could not be otherwise: One cannot, by definition, wage a military (and not metaphorical) war against terrorism, for the terrorists themselves are not waging a war. Wars are fought to coerce an enemy to accept one's policies or sovereignty. Even when they involve the mass slaughter of civilians—as has been increasingly the case since World War I—they are not terrorism. (A Palestinian suicide bombing, however repulsive, is the act of a civilian combatant in a war of independence.) Terrorism is committed by small, clandestine, independent groups—the evil twins of NGOs—in the attempt to persuade like-minded people to join their side, whether physically or intellectually. The massacre at the World Trade Center was, in terms of the United States, a means without an end: There were no grounds on which the US could admit "defeat"; the only possible "victory" for al Qaeda was a sympathetic response from within the Muslim world.

In a revenge-seeking and deliberate confusion of host and guest, the US military easily overthrew the essentially unarmed Taliban regime, leaving vast areas of the country in the hands of warlords, and partially restoring the freedoms (music and television, women without burqas and girls in school, clean shaven men) which the Afghans had enjoyed under that oppressive Soviet occupation the US, through its fundamentalist surrogates, the Taliban, had fought so long. (Freedom, however, only goes so far: A few days ago, a political cartoonist was thrown in prison for mildly satirizing President Karzai.) The country is in ruins, but the pipeline from Kazakhstan has now become a reality, and its plans are drawn, the fulfillment of an old dream among the Bush crowd. As Dick Cheney said in 1998, when he was CEO of Halliburton:

> I can't think of a time when we've had a region emerge as suddenly to become as strategically significant as the Caspian. It's almost as if the opportunities have arisen overnight. The good Lord didn't see fit to put oil and gas only where there are democratically elected regimes friendly to the United States. Occasionally we have to operate in places where, all things considered, one would not normally choose to go. But we go where the business is.

The War on Terrorism has been good for business, but hasn't done anything bad against the terrorists. With one possible exception (an Egyptian strategic planner), not a single important al Qaeda member has been killed or captured. George Bush has not mentioned the name "Osama bin Laden" in six or eight months, and no wonder: He may think he's Wyatt Earp, but those evil-doing Clanton Brothers aren't playing by the rules and they never showed up at the OK Corral. So all Bush can do is just shoot at anybody who looks mean.

After all, al Qaeda—once one strips away the propaganda—appears to be a group of, at most, a few hundred educated, middle class fanatics, who masterminded terrorist actions, mainly in Africa, at the rate of one every eighteen months. They also ran camps in Afghanistan for thousands of young peasants attracted to local jihads, including 5,000 trained by Pakistani intelligence for incursions into Kashmir and 3,000 Uzbekis attempting to overthrow the dictatorship in Uzbekistan (which receives hundreds of millions of dollars in US military aid). It is these Afghan and foreign peasants, Taliban foot soldiers and jihadis, that the Bush Team has labeled "al Qaeda terrorists" and left to rot in Guantanamo Bay (in cages, by the way, identical to the one in which Ezra Pound was placed in Pisa in 1945). Al Qaeda, as the recent bombings in Kenya prove, continues as it did before. Forced out of Afghanistan, it is merely less visible.

There is indeed a malevolent "sleeper cell" in the United States, but it is not the one in Attorney General John Ashcroft's apocalyptic imagination. It was formed in the 1970s, in the Ford Administration, by Donald Rumsfeld, then as now Secretary of Defense, and his young disciple, Dick Cheney, whom Rumsfeld got appointed as White House Chief of Staff. During the Reagan years they attracted brilliant young ideological extremists: Paul Wolfowitz, Richard Perle, Eliott Abrams, Zalmay Khalilzad, among them. In 1992, the last year of the Bush Sr. administration, convinced, as everyone was, that Bush would be reelected, and hoping for a second-term purge of the multilateralists surrounding the President, they launched their first secret manifesto: "Defense Planning Guidance for the Fiscal Years 1994-1999," written by Wolfowitz and Khalilzad, under the direction of then Secretary of Defense Cheney.

According to their "Guidance," with the collapse of the Soviet Union, the "first objective" of the United States was now "to prevent the re-emergence [sic] of a new rival":

> The US must show the leadership necessary to establish and protect a new order that holds the promise of convincing potential competitors that they need not aspire to a greater role.
>
> [We must] discourage [the] advanced industrial nations [from] challenging our leadership.
>
> We must maintain the mechanisms for deterring potential competitors from even aspiring to a larger regional or global role.
>
> We will retain the preeminent responsibility for addressing... those wrongs which threaten our interests.... Various types of US interests may be involved in such instances: access to vital raw materials, primarily Persian Gulf oil; proliferation of weapons of mass destruction and ballistic missiles, threats to US citizens from terrorism...

The report, which never mentioned any allies in these global efforts, was an embarrassment to Bush Sr. and his consensus-building advisers, and was quickly suppressed after it was leaked to the *New York Times*. Then Bush was defeated by Clinton, and the cell went underground in the boardrooms of corporations and right-wing foundations and think tanks.

In 1997, "appalled by the incoherent policies of the Clinton administration," they formed a group called the Project for the New American Century (PNAC), "to make the case and rally support for American global leadership" and to restore "military strength and moral clarity." Their founding statement was signed by, among others, Rumsfeld, Cheney, Wolfowitz, Khalilzad, Lewis Libby, and Jeb Bush (at the time the Heir Apparent), along with such imams of conservatism as Francis Fukuyama, William Bennett, and Norman Podhoretz.

In September 2000—when the election of Gore seemed a certainty—PNAC produced what was to become the Hammurabic Code of the Bush Jr. Administration: *Rebuilding America's Defenses: Strategies, Forces and Resources for a New Century*. The document, which is endless, speaks openly of a "Pax Americana": expanding current US military bases abroad, and building new ones in the Middle East, Southeast Europe, Latin America, and Southeast Asia. It is contemptuous of the United Nations. It recommends "pre-emptive strikes" and particularly mentions Iraq, Iran, and North Korea. It suggests that to fight these countries we need small nuclear warheads to target "very deep, underground bunkers." (Such weapons, called Robust Nuclear Earth Penetrators, are now being developed.) It speaks of fighting and "decisively winning simultaneous major theater wars." (Thus Rumsfeld's current obsession with taking on Iraq and North Korea at the same time.) It is the origin of that bizarre, Teutonic phrase, "homeland security." It advocates, as has now been done, pulling out of the Anti-Ballistic Missile and all other international defense treaties—in the Pax Americana we won't need them. It recommends increasing defense spending to 3.8% of the Gross Domestic Product (the amount of the 2003 budget, almost to the penny). It talks not only of controlling outer space with Star Wars weaponry, but also of controlling cyberspace, fighting "enemies" (foreign or domestic?) on the Internet. One of its many charts reads:

	Cold War	21st Century
Security System:	Bipolar	Unipolar
Strategic Goal:	Contain Soviet Union	Preserve Pax Americana
Main Military Mission(s):	Deter Soviet expansion	Secure and expand zones of democratic peace; deter rise of new great-power competitors; defend key regions; exploit transformation of war
Main Military Threat(s):	Potential global war across many theaters	Potential theater wars spread across globe
Focus of Strategic Competition:	Europe	East Asia

The US, in short, is "the essential defender of today's global security order." Allies are unnecessary; world opinion is irrelevant; potential competitors must be crushed early. And, in the eeriest moment in the report, it imagines "some catastrophic event," a "new Pearl Harbor," that will be the catalyst for the US to decisively launch its new Pax. (Small wonder that, on September 12, 2001, Donald Rumsfeld insisted we immediately invade Iraq and, shortly after,

Condoleezza Rice convened senior members of the National Security Council to ask them to "think about 'How do you capitalize on these opportunities?'")

The Sleeper Cell has awoken. After successfully engineering a judicial coup d'etat to install their genial figurehead as President, they now control the US government. Led by Cheney and Rumsfeld, Wolfowitz is Deputy Defense Secretary, Khalilzad is Ambassador to Afghanistan, Libby is Cheney's chief of staff, Abrams (after having been disgraced in the Iran-contra scandal, and after years campaigning for a law to require the posting of the Ten Commandments in every government building) is now chief White House adviser on the Middle East. A half-dozen others from PNAC hold important posts in the Defense and State departments. Their goal has been cheerfully described by Condoleezza Rice (who believes that Bush is "someone of tremendous intellect"): "American foreign policy in a Republican administration should refocus the United States on the national interest. There is nothing wrong with doing something that benefits all humanity, but that is, in a sense, a second order effect." Richard Perle, chairman of the Defense Policy Board, is more honest: "This is total war... If we just let our vision of the world go forth, and we embrace it entirely and we don't try to piece together clever diplomacy, but just wage a total war, our children will sing great songs about us years from now."

In ways that Ronald Reagan would envy, the Sleeper Cell is masterful at manipulating the new forms of mass media, particularly the hyperbolic television news and radio talk shows. It officially began the rhetorical invasion of Iraq precisely on September 1 (in the words of Andrew Card, White House chief of staff, "You don't launch a new product in August") and was relentless in creating frightening stories until the November elections. Endless reports of atrocities committed by Saddam Hussein (some of them, of course, true) were combined with assertions that, as Rumsfeld put it, there is "bulletproof evidence" linking Saddam and al Qaeda (none of which has ever been produced), which in turn were combined with frequent warnings from Ashcroft and the FBI and the CIA of new "spectacular attacks" from al Qaeda "that meet several criteria: high symbolic value, mass casualties, severe damage to the American economy and maximum psychological trauma."

It is dizzying trying to keep up with the news, to remember what happened the day before—which is precisely their intention—but let two examples suffice: In December, a few days after Iraq turned over a 12,000 page list of their weapons to the UN—an act first demanded by the White House, then ridiculed when Iraq complied, then partially suppressed when it revealed the names of too many US corporations that had been helping Iraq all along—the media were suddenly flooded with a story that Iraq had given al Qaeda the nerve gas VX, an odorless, colorless oil that causes death in minutes. This story, needless to say, fit all the criteria for sensational news: Iraq/al Qaeda connection, gruesome death, and terrorist threat. A few days later, those omnipresent and anonymous "senior officials" were telling CNN that there was "absolutely no intelligence" on this matter, "zero confirmation of evidence." Obviously the story had originally come from the government, and it followed the classic pattern of what was, during the Vietnam War, called "disinformation": leak false information, wait until it has its effect, and then deny it, knowing that assertions remain in the collective memory longer than their negations.

Far more serious is the current frenzy over the possibility that Iraq will somehow release smallpox, either among American troops in the projected war, or in the US itself through its imagined terrorist surrogates. This has led to the mass production of smallpox vaccines—to the delight of the drug company executives in the Bush inner circle—ambitious plans to vaccinate the entire country and the predictable "lifeboat" debates on television of who should be vaccinated first.

The smallpox panic largely comes from the assertions of Judith Miller, a *New York Times* reporter, that unnamed "intelligence sources" are "investigating" whether a scientist named Nelja Maltseva from the Russian Institute of Viral Preparations visited Baghdad in 1990 and sold Iraq a vial of a smallpox strain that caused an epidemic in Kazakhstan in 1972.

Dr. Maltseva died two years ago. Both her daughter and a laboratory assistant claim that she only visited Iraq once, in 1971, as part of a global smallpox eradication effort, and that her last trip abroad was to Finland in 1982. Furthermore, the Russians have always claimed that the Kazakhstan epidemic never happened, but was merely Cold War propaganda.

Edward Said attacked Miller years ago for her "thesis about the militant, hateful quality of the Arab world." Among her many books, she is the co-author of *Saddam Hussein and the Crisis in the Gulf* with Laurie Mylroie, who is the author of *Saddam Hussein's Unfinished War Against America*, which expounds the theory that Saddam personally orchestrated the 1993 World Trade Center bombing—a theory that only Richard Perle seems to believe ("splendid and convincing"). Like almost everyone on the White House Team, Miller is associated with two right wing think tanks, the American Enterprise Institute for Public Policy Research (the latest issue of its magazine features Oriana Fallaci on the "moral superiority of Western culture") and the Middle East Forum, which has been posting the names of university professors critical of Bush on its website. The Forum is run by Daniel Pipes, who is famous for his comment about the "massive immigration of brown-skinned peoples cooking strange foods and not exactly maintaining Germanic standards of hygiene."

The general hysteria about smallpox, in other words, and the very real possibility of mass vaccinations with its statistically inevitable corresponding deaths, is entirely the result of unsubstantiated rumors published by someone with a clear agenda.

Meanwhile, over at the Pentagon, Rumsfeld has created 2POG, the $7 billion Proactive Pre-emptive Operations Group, whose "super-intelligence support activity" will combine "CIA and military covert action, information warfare, and deception." Along with the usual boys' magazine fantasies of high-tech espionage (including something about "tagging" the clothes of terrorists with DNA samples that can be perceived by laser beams from satellites) the "proactive" component consists of "duping al Qaeda into undertaking operations it is not prepared for and thereby exposing its personnel." That is, encouraging terrorist acts that will provoke an American response. If this seems unimaginable, or paranoid, it is worth remembering Operation Northwoods, which the Pentagon proposed to Kennedy a few months before he was assassinated. The idea then was a project of bombings, hijackings and plane crashes that would kill American citizens and lead to popular sentiment for an invasion of Cuba. (Kennedy—even James Bond-addicted Kennedy— rejected that one.)

Around another bend of the Pentagon, the Defense Research Projects Agency has created the Information Awareness Office, whose mission is "Total Information Awareness" (TIA). The Office is run by retired Admiral John Poindexter, who in 1990 was convicted of five felony counts for lying to Congress about the Iran-contra affair. TIA, according to Poindexter, will create "ultra large-scale, semantically rich, easily implementable database technologies" that will allow the Pentagon to access "world-wide, distributed, legacy databases as if they were one centralized database." Which means: every possible computerized record in the US, on which an individual's name appears, will be copied and collated by the Pentagon: credit card purchases, library books, police records, automatic toll-collectors on bridges, university course enlistments, membership lists, and on and on—as well as all e-mails and logs of Internet surfing. They have received $200 million for a pilot program. Over the door of Poindexter's office is the motto "Scientia Est Potentia," Knowledge Is Power. (George Bush presumably being the exception that proves the rule.)

The Sleeper Cell has awoken, and there is nothing to stop them. The Democratic Party, afraid of being branded "unpatriotic" by the Republicans, has gone into hibernation. The tattered remains of the Left is—as the Left always is—more preoccupied with fighting among themselves. With a few individual exceptions, there is almost no opposition in the major media. (Powerful anti-Bush articles by, among others, Gore Vidal, Harold Pinter, John Le Carré, and John Berger, are published in England, but not here.) The only forum for criticism is the Internet, which, though still uncontrolled, remains the one point in the PNAC program that has yet to be (openly) addressed by the Bush Team. As we enter Bush II Anno III, anger has turned into a kind of sullen resignation.

Perhaps the problem is that there are no words to describe this Administration. All the pejoratives, however accurate, that might be applied—"warmongerers" and "imperialists," "corrupt" and "bloodthirsty," "fanatical" and "criminal"—have been drained of their meaning by decades of propaganda. They are as banal as the rhetoric of the think tanks. Small wonder that American writers have generally been either silent or bathetic ("9/11 reminded me of the day my father died") on all that has happened in the last two years. We no longer have the words to even think about what is happening, about violence that is not "just like a movie," about people like Cheney and Rumsfeld and Perle and Wolfowitz and Rice and

Ashcroft and Bush, who are not Pol Pot or Stalin or Hitler, who are lesser forms of evil, but evil nonetheless. To begin to talk about them is to relive the old nightmare of the scream with no sound. ■

Look for these titles by Prickly Paradigm, and others to come: